RUSSIAN IMMIGRANTS
IN THEIR SHOES

BY BARBARA KRASNER

Published by The Child's World®
1980 Lookout Drive • Mankato, MN 56003-1705
800-599-READ • www.childsworld.com

Content Consultant: Tatiana Osipovich, Associate Professor of Russian, Lewis & Clark College

Photographs ©: Iakov Filimonov/Shutterstock Images, cover, 1; AP Images, 6, 8, 9, 26; Berliner Verlag/Archiv/picture-alliance/dpa/AP Images, 10; Konrad Giehr/picture-alliance/dpa/AP Images, 12; Red Line Editorial, 13, 22; Dina Makarova/AP Images, 14, 16; Andrea Comas/Reuters/Newscom, 17; Juan Carlos Rojas/Notimex/Newscom, 18; Baltel/Sipa/Newscom, 20; M. Zhazo/Hindustan Times/Newscom, 21; Shutterstock Images, 24, 27; Boris Yurchenko/AP Images, 28

ISBN 9781503828018
LCCN 2018944223

Printed in the United States of America
PA02394

ABOUT THE AUTHOR

Barbara Krasner is the author of more than 30 books for young readers. She teaches American immigrant history at several New Jersey universities.

TABLE OF CONTENTS

FAST FACTS

Information on Russia

- In the late 1800s and early 1900s, Jews in Russia were attacked by non-Jewish people. Many Jews left Russia because of this.

- Russia is the largest country by land mass in the world.

- After the Russian **Revolution** of 1917, Russia fell under **Communist** control. In December 1922, it became the Union of Soviet Socialist **Republics**. It was also known as the Soviet Union.

- In 1991, the Soviet Union collapsed, and all 15 former republics (including Russia) became independent states.

Important Numbers

- Approximately 3.1 million Americans claim Russian heritage.

- In 1910, 65,000 Russians lived in the United States.

- Nearly 14,000 Russians arrived in the United States between 1916 and 1920. Another 22,662 immigrants came between 1921 and 1927.

TIMELINE

1917–1921: A Russian civil war between Communists and anti-Communists breaks out. Many Russians flee the Communist **regime** in what is often called the first wave of Russian **emigration**.

1922: The Soviet Union forms.

1945–1950s: A second wave of emigrants leaves the Soviet Union after World War II (1939–1945). Many of them seek new lives in the United States.

1945–1991: The **Cold War** between the United States and the Soviet Union takes place. This restricts emigration from the Soviet Union to the United States.

1970–1980s: A third wave of emigration from the Soviet Union begins.

1990s: What is sometimes called the fourth wave of emigration from Russia and other former republics of the Soviet Union takes place.

1991: The Soviet Union collapses, and all 15 republics become independent states.

Chapter 1

STEAMING TO THE UNITED STATES

Golda Mabovitch waited every day for a letter from her father. She wanted to read the words: Here are your tickets! Join me in the United States! When her father left her, her two sisters, and her mother in 1903 to find work in the United States, they did not know how long they would have to wait. Finally, the letter came in 1905. He was living in a place called Milwaukee, Wisconsin.

◄ **Golda Mabovitch studied at the Milwaukee Normal School, which is now the University of Wisconsin-Milwaukee.**

Golda's family was Jewish. They decided to leave Russia because there was widespread anti-Jewish violence happening there. They had to say goodbye to family and friends. In early 1906, train-station farewells erupted into tearful hugs.

The family's first stop was the Austria-Hungary border. To cross, Golda's mother had to bribe policemen, Golda remembered, "with money [she] had somehow managed to raise."[1] Golda was grateful when her family was able to cross the border. Once in Austria-Hungary, the family shivered in the icy spring morning, waiting in a shack for their train to Antwerp, Belgium.

They waited more once they arrived in Belgium. In an immigration center, Golda and her family had to wait another 48 hours before they could board a steamship. Golda was anxious. She wanted to see her father.

"Going to America then was almost like going to the moon."[2]

—*Golda (Mabovitch) Meir*

▲ As Israel's prime minster, Golda met with President Richard Nixon.

Golda later recalled, "It was not a pleasure trip, that fourteen-day journey aboard ship. Crammed into a dark, stuffy cabin with four other people, we spent the nights on sheetless bunks and most of the days standing in line for food that was ladled out to us as though we were cattle."[3]

To Golda, all immigrants looked alike: pale, tired, and frightened, just like her. She passed the time by sharing dreams with other children about the riches they would find in the United States.

Golda's father met the family at the Milwaukee train station in an automobile. Golda had never ridden in one before. She didn't recognize her father because he no longer wore a beard.

Her father didn't recognize Golda because her clothes had no shape or color. Golda loved her new American clothes, soda pop, and ice cream. She loved her first time in a skyscraper, five stories high. She remembered, "I stood for hours staring at the traffic and the people."[4]

Golda became a top student in her poor immigrant neighborhood. Her father got work as a railway carpenter, and her mother ran a grocery. Golda eventually moved to Palestine. She went on to become Israel's prime minister in 1969.

▲ **As an adult, Golda worked in politics.**

Chapter 2

ESCAPING COMMUNISM

In 1946, two-year-old George Derugin gripped his mother's hand. They raced alongside George's father on the platform to catch the last train out of Berlin, Germany's capital. They had to leave the city before the Soviet tanks arrived. There were 26 children on the train, most shivering from the cold and starving. At the end of World War II, the victorious forces divided Germany into four sections. Berlin fell into the Soviet section.

◄ The Soviet Union controlled the eastern part of Germany after World War II.

As the Soviets approached to claim their sector in 1946, George's parents decided to leave. They felt that although much of the city of Berlin already suffered from lack of food, it would only get worse with the Communists in charge.

Fleeing from their home was not new to the Derugin family. George's grandfather, a member of the Russian Parliament, had been forced to leave Russia during the Russian Revolution in 1917 because he was anti-Communist. He traveled first to Finland and then settled in Germany. George's father was born in Russia's capital city of Saint Petersburg in 1915. He later became a professor at a university in Berlin. He stayed there throughout World War II.

The Derugins traveled to Munich, a city in the American zone of Germany. But George's family wanted to leave Europe. They believed the farther they could get from Europe, the safer they'd feel. They chose to go to the United States.

The Derugins arrived in New York City in the early 1950s. They didn't stay in New York long. George's father found a position as a professor at the University of Southern California. The family moved to Los Angeles, California.

▲ **The Soviet Union built a wall in Berlin. They didn't want people in East Berlin to cross into West Berlin.**

But other children were cruel to George there. At the time of his arrival, Americans were scared of the spread of Communism. Children called George cruel names because of his Russian background. The family eventually moved.

They went to the San Francisco, California, area. As an adult, George became a vice president in a banking business. He is proud to speak Russian nearly fluently. His children also speak Russian.

MAP OF THE SOVIET UNION

The Soviet Union had 15 republics in its final years.

Chapter 3

A DANCER DEFECTS

On the night of June 29, 1974, ballet dancer Mikhail Baryshnikov tightened the belt around his striped robe and fiddled with his mustard-yellow scarf. His heart beat faster than when he was leaping in the air on stage. He took off the robe and scarf and moved through the back of the theater to take his position. He had to dance well tonight. This would be his last performance as a Soviet dancer.

This performance at a Toronto theater in Canada was the last stop for the Soviet dance company he was part of. With each turn and each leap, he moved closer to freedom. When the applause stopped and the curtains closed, Baryshnikov hurried to the back of the theater and out the door. His lawyer was waiting for him in a getaway car. They took off. Baryshnikov glanced back at the theater through the car's windows. His heart pounded quickly.

Baryshnikov **defected** from the Soviet Union. If anyone caught him, he could lose his citizenship. He could face prison time. The idea to defect came from his American friends. He later said, "I just got the message from my closest friends . . . that if I have any doubts and if I want to stay [in the United States], they will help me."[5] His friends set him up with a lawyer.

Baryshnikov knew for his own personal and creative freedom, the Soviet Union offered few opportunities. Yet he was taking a huge risk. As the car sped away, Baryshnikov worried about his stepfather, stepbrother, and stepsister. He said, "I knew that they would be under the scrutiny of [Soviet state security], of course."[6] One month later, he joined the American Ballet Theatre in New York City. He became an international dance sensation.

Baryshnikov was invited into the homes of some famous musicians and other celebrities who became his good friends. He learned English by watching American television. In 1986, he became a U.S. citizen.

▲ **Baryshnikov danced with Gelsey Kirkland while in the American Ballet Theatre.**

▲ **Baryshnikov inspired many dancers through his work.**

Baryshnikov started his own dance company and gained a legendary reputation as a dancer, choreographer, and performer. Leaving the Soviet Union allowed him to pursue his artistic dreams.

Chapter 4

EXIT VISAS

As his parents packed three orange suitcases and two olive-green sacks, six-year-old Igor Shteyngart poked through their apartment's curtains to peer out the window. A thick frost covered all the signs on the street. It was 1977. No one said where they were going, but the apartment they lived in had been sold to the son of a Communist Party official. The man was eager to get ahold of it.

◄ **Igor Shteyngart, known as author Gary Shteyngart, has written multiple books as an adult.**

At the airport, a crowd of aunts and cousins surrounded Igor and his parents to say their goodbyes. Only then did Igor sense he was leaving the country. He and his parents flew from Leningrad in the Soviet Union to East Berlin in East Germany. Then they took another plane to Vienna, Austria, and then to Rome, Italy.

Igor later learned that leaving the Soviet Union meant his family would be considered traitors. His parents didn't tell him where they were going because they feared he would reveal their secret. Although Igor's father had **exit visas** for them, if anyone leaked their destination, the visas would be canceled.

"The army-green sacks are too heavy for a child, or a mama, to lift, but I push them forward with a kick whenever I can to help out my family. The instincts that will see me through my life are stirring for the first time: forward, move forward, keep going, keep kicking."[7]

—*Igor Shteyngart as he left Russia*

19

▲ Igor's written works have won many awards.

▲ **Igor has written books about his immigrant experience.**

In Italy, Igor continued to wear a polka-dot shirt from the Soviet Union. But over it he now wore a new Italian sweater. When he lived in the Soviet Union, he had rings under his eyes. In Italy, he got the sleep and fresh air he needed to breathe freely.

The family of three visited different museums and churches. In their apartment, Igor began to collect books written in English.

WHERE RUSSIAN IMMIGRANTS LIVED AS OF 2015

Country	Number of Russian Immigrants
Ukraine	1.9 million
Kazakhstan	1.2 million
Germany	606,000
Uzbekistan	474,000
Belarus	377,000
United States	206,000
Tajikistan	135,000
Estonia	90,000
Latvia	88,000
Kyrgyzstan	68,000
Israel	66,000
Italy	63,000

His father's mother, Grandma Polya, and her husband, Grandpa Ilya, joined them. The family stayed in Italy for five months. He finally learned that they were all going to the United States. Igor thought, "We are going to the enemy."[8]

Ever since the end of World War II, the United States and the Soviet Union were hostile toward each other. Igor had been taught in the Soviet Union that the United States was an enemy.

But in 1979, Igor, his parents, and grandparents boarded a plane that would take them to New York City. Igor pressed his nose against the window as the plane landed. Buildings taller than any he had ever seen before seemed to fill the window. He was now seven years old. He felt as if his entire life in the Soviet Union had been all gray. Now, in the United States, there was color. Once out of the airport, he rode in a car that was three times as big as those back home. This American car seemed to float in the air.

The Shteyngarts settled in Queens, New York. Igor took the name Gary to sound like an American. He became a popular writer in the United States. He wrote about being Russian, "My parents and grandparents never fully recovered from the strains of having lived in an **authoritarian** society. . . . They left Russia, but Russia never left them."[9]

Chapter 5

AFTER THE FALL

Dr. Alex Feoktistov walked quickly down the hospital hallway. He passed rooms where sick patients rested in beds, and he greeted nearby nurses. It was 1990 and just another day for Feoktistov at the hospital in Riga, Latvia. But then he received a phone call during his shift. He knew something must be happening for this friend to call him at work. He picked up the phone and heard his friend's familiar voice.

◄ **Riga became the capital of Latvia in 1918.**

His friend, who had government connections, warned him that change was coming to Latvia.

Although Feoktistov had lived most of his life in Latvia, he was born in Russia. At the time, both republics belonged to the Soviet Union. His wife, Masha, was a dentist. She had come to Latvia 12 years before. The couple lived in an apartment. Now Feoktistov's friend said anyone who had not lived in Latvia for the last 16 years would no longer be allowed to own an apartment.

Latvians wanted to lead their own country. Feoktistov said, "Everyone who was not Latvian became unwelcome in the republic."[10] As the Soviet Union began to crumble in 1990, Latvian leadership became possible. That didn't bode well for Feoktistov and his wife, who were not Latvian by birth. When Feoktistov came home that night, he said to Masha, "Let's go to America."[11] Much to his surprise, she quickly agreed.

"When we came to America—our first months here—we were in a state of shock. . . . We didn't understand what we had done. We had burned all our bridges."[12]

—Alex Feoktistov

▲ **People in Latvia demanded independence from the Soviet Union in 1990.**

Feoktistov called friends in New York. One friend cheerfully encouraged him to move. But another friend warned him that it could be tough living in the United States. Feoktistov and Masha decided to go. After selling the apartment, Feoktistov and Masha had just enough money for one exit visa. Feoktistov had to travel to Moscow, Russia, to get it. He and his wife would not be able to emigrate together.

▲ St. Basil's Cathedral in Moscow is one of the most famous
buildings in Russia.

▲ **In late 1991, Soviet President Mikhail Gorbachev announced the end of the Soviet Union.**

One month after they agreed to leave, Feoktistov was on a plane to New York. Meanwhile, Masha sold all their belongings. In two months she was able to get her own exit visa. By that time, Latvia had already declared its intent to gain independence from the Soviet Union. Masha arrived in New York in March 1991.

With no money, they took whatever jobs they could. Their only goal was to survive. But they felt that they were in charge of their own lives. No one told them what to do. Feoktistov was able to practice medicine and work as a doctor. In 2018, he was working at a medical center in Brooklyn, New York.

THINK ABOUT IT

- Some Russian scientists, artists, and dancers took a great risk in leaving everyone and everything they knew to emigrate from the Soviet Union and begin a new life in the United States. In their position, do you think you would have chosen to emigrate?
- Why do you think the Soviet Union didn't want people to move to the United States?
- Do you think it was difficult for Russian families to leave their home country? Explain your answer.

GLOSSARY

authoritarian (uh-thor-i-TAIR-ee-uhn): An authoritarian society is one in which people are expected to be obedient to the government at the cost of their freedom. In the Soviet Union, authoritarian leaders dictated the actions of their citizens.

Cold War (KOHLD WOR): A Cold War occurs when two countries are politically hostile toward one another. The United States and Soviet Union were in a Cold War from 1947 to 1991.

Communist (KOM-yuh-nist): Communist describes an economic, political, and social system controlled by the state. In the Communist Soviet Union, all property belonged to the state and there was only one political party: the Communist Party.

defected (dih-FEK-ted): Defected means to leave one's country for another, opposing country. Some citizens of the Soviet Union defected to the United States.

emigration (em-i-GREY-shun): Emigration is the act of leaving one's country. The Cold War hindered emigration from the Soviet Union to the United States.

exit visas (EK-sit VEE-suz): Exit visas are documents that show permission for a person to leave a country. The Shteyngart family needed exit visas to leave the Soviet Union.

regime (reh-ZSHEEM): A regime is a government that is in control of people for a period of time. Some Russians left during the Communist regime.

republics (ri-PUHB-likz): Republics are places that have a form of government where people can elect representatives to serve in the government. The republics in the Soviet Union didn't have many candidate choices when voting in elections.

revolution (rev-uh-LOO-shun): A revolution is an event in which a group takes over a government. The Russian Revolution happened in 1917.

SOURCE NOTES

1. Golda Meir. *My Life*. London, UK: Weidenfeld and Nicolson, 1975. Print. 14.

2. Ibid. 14.

3. Ibid. 15.

4. Ibid. 17.

5. "Interview with Mikhail Baryshnikov." *CNN*. Cable News Network, 5 May 2002. Web. 10 July 2018.

6. Ibid.

7. Gary Shteyngart. *Little Failure*. New York, NY: Random House, 2014. Print. 82.

8. Ibid. 83.

9. Gary Shteyngart. "Living in Trump's Soviet Union." *New Yorker*. Condé Nast, 21 Nov. 2016. Web. 10 July 2018.

10. Dennis Elliott Shasha. *Red Blues: Voices from the Last Wave of Russian Immigrants*. New York, NY: Holmes & Meier, 2002. Print. 140.

11. Ibid. 141.

12. Ibid. 144.

TO LEARN MORE

Books

Centore, Michael. *Russia*. Broomall, PA: Mason Crest, 2015.

Otfinoski, Steven. *The Cold War*. New York, NY: Scholastic, 2018.

Yomtov, Nelson. *Russia*. New York, NY: Children's Press, 2012.

Web Sites

Visit our Web site for links about Russian immigrants:
childsworld.com/links

Note to Parents, Teachers, and Librarians: We routinely verify our Web links to make sure they are safe and active sites. So encourage your readers to check them out!

INDEX